TIME FOR KIDS READERS

WE ARE VIRGINIA

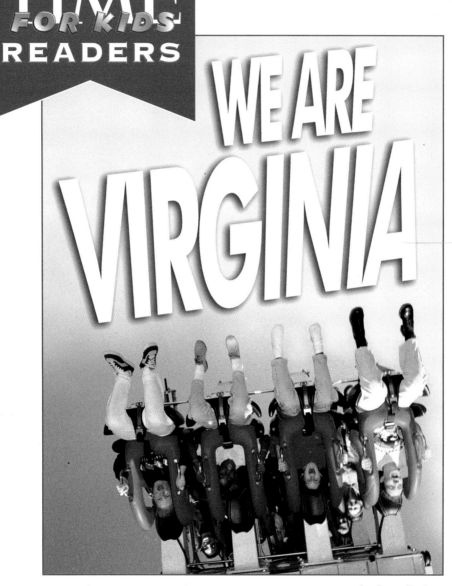

by Anna Prokos

Harcourt

Orlando   Austin   Chicago   New York   Toronto   London   San Diego

Visit *The Learning Site!*
www.harcourtschool.com

Who lives in Virginia? Lots of people. More than 7,078,515 people call this state home, according to the results of Census 2000 conducted by the United States Census Bureau. The census is a study made every 10 years. It tells how many and what kinds of people live in the United States. It tells where people live and gives some information about their lives. The census also collects information about the population of every state.

The results of the census are put to good use. For example, the number of representatives each state has in the United States House of Representatives is based on population. If a state's population has increased since the last census, the state may get more representatives. If a state's population has decreased, so may its number of representatives. The census may show that a state has a growing number of children. That means the state might need to build more schools.

The census of Virginia has given us some important results. Since 1990, Virginia's population has grown. Virginia is now ranked number 12 in population of all the 50 states. That means more and more people have moved to Virginia or were born in the state between 1990 and 2000.

2

FAST FACTS

Capital:	Richmond
Largest city:	Virginia Beach (425,257 people)
Largest county by population:	Fairfax (969,749 people)
Motto:	*Sic semper tyrannis* (Thus always to tyrants)
State flower:	Flowering dogwood
State bird:	Cardinal
State dog:	American foxhound
State shell:	Oyster shell
State tree:	Flowering dogwood
Nicknames:	Old Dominion; Mother of Presidents; Mother of States

SOURCE: Time Almanac 2002

FAST FACTS

- Virginia was settled by English immigrants starting in 1607.

- The largest group in Virginia is of German ancestry. It has about 828,000 people.

- British ancestry is a close second to German. About 789,000 people in Virginia say they have ancestors from Britain.

- About 696,000 people have Irish ancestry.

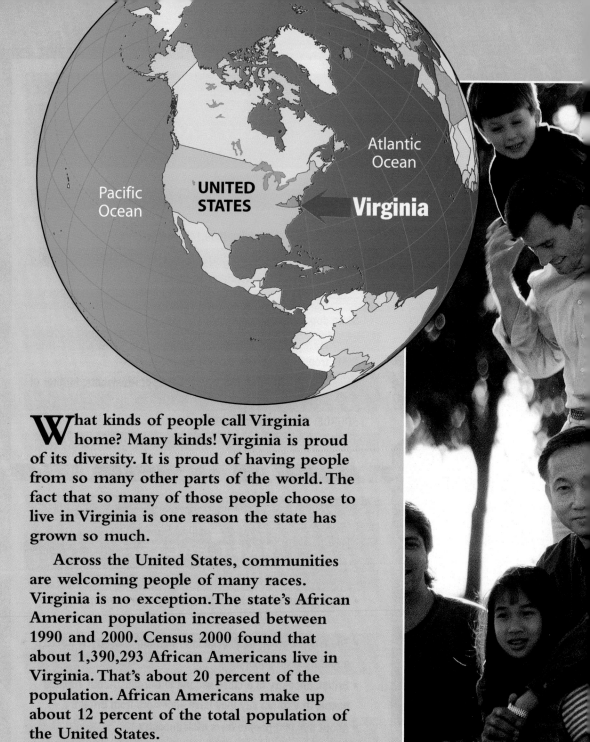

What kinds of people call Virginia home? Many kinds! Virginia is proud of its diversity. It is proud of having people from so many other parts of the world. The fact that so many of those people choose to live in Virginia is one reason the state has grown so much.

Across the United States, communities are welcoming people of many races. Virginia is no exception. The state's African American population increased between 1990 and 2000. Census 2000 found that about 1,390,293 African Americans live in Virginia. That's about 20 percent of the population. African Americans make up about 12 percent of the total population of the United States.

The fastest-growing group in Virginia—as in the rest of the United States—is Hispanic people. As people from Spanish-speaking countries, such as the Dominican Republic and Mexico, move to Virginia, the number of Hispanic people increases. Virginia's Hispanic population more than doubled between 1990 and 2000. According to Census 2000, about 5 percent of Virginians are Hispanics. That's 5 out of every 100 people. In the entire United States, Hispanics make up about 12 percent of the population.

Which area of Virginia has the greatest diversity? Northern Virginia is the most diverse area of the state. That area is made up of Arlington, Fairfax, Loudoun, and Prince William Counties. It also includes the cities of Alexandria, Arlington, Fairfax, Falls Church, Manassas, and Manassas Park. People from almost every racial and ethnic group live in northern Virginia.

Playing street hockey is one way to have fun in Ashburn, a city in Loudoun County.

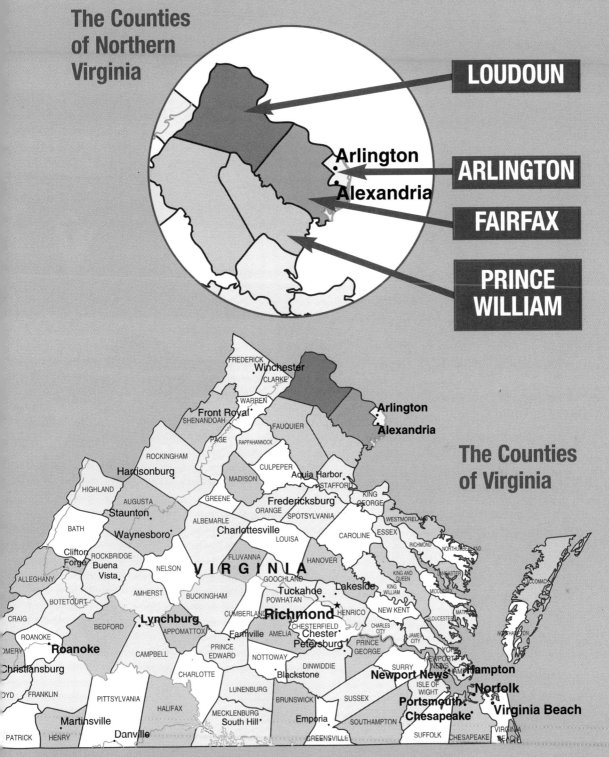

The Counties of Northern Virginia

LOUDOUN

ARLINGTON

FAIRFAX

PRINCE WILLIAM

Arlington

Alexandria

The Counties of Virginia

Since the 1940s, immigrants have moved to Falls Church, Virginia, because of its housing, jobs, and transportation. People came to the city, located in Fairfax County, from countries all over the world. Today one-third of the students living in Fairfax County speak a language other than English at home. In Falls Church, Bailey's Elementary School is a good example of Virginia's diversity. The parents of many students moved to Virginia from countries such as Cuba, Somalia, Pakistan, Mexico, Saudi Arabia, Iran, and El Salvador.

Bailey's Elementary isn't the only school that is proud of its racial and ethnic diversity. In the city of Alexandria, the Francis C. Hammond Middle School has an international club as part of its after-school program. The club helps students learn about different cultures, races, and countries. Of about 1,290 students, 45 percent are African American, nearly 28 percent are Hispanic, about 17 percent are white, more than 9 percent are of Asian Pacific heritage, and less than 1 percent are Native Americans.

First graders at Bailey's Elementary School.

A person may be considered part of more than one racial group if his or her parents, grandparents, or other ancestors came from two different countries, cultures, or races.

Census 2000 was the first one in which people could identify themselves as being of two or more races. In Virginia and in the United States, most people told the census that they belong to one group. However, some people said that they belong to more than one race. These people consider themselves multiethnic or multiracial.

Experts who study populations predict that the number of multiracial Americans will grow to 30 million by the year 2050. In Census 2000, most of the people who identified themselves as multiracial were under 30 years old. About 2 percent of Virginia's population identified themselves this way in 2000.

TFK FAST FACTS

Final Count: How does Virginia's population compare with the rest of the United States?

	VA	USA
Population in 2000	7,078,515	281,421,906
Children under 5 years old	6.5 %	6.8%
Children under 18	24.6%	25.7%
People aged 65 and over	11.2%	12.4%
Female	51%	50.9%
Caucasians	72.3%	75.1%
African American	19.6%	12.3%
Hispanic	4.7%	12.5%
Asian	3.7%	3.6%
Native American/Alaska Native	0.3%	0.9%
Native Hawaiian/Other Pacific Islander	0.1%	0.1%
Other race	2%	5.5%
People reporting two or more races	2%	2.4%

SOURCE: United States Census Bureau

11

In Virginia, some areas have more multiracial people than others. Most multiracial Virginians live in the two regions of the state that have large cities. Those areas are northern Virginia and the Tidewater region.

The Tidewater area of Virginia includes Virginia Beach and Norfolk, where the U.S. Navy has a large base. The Tidewater's population is about two-thirds white and one-third African American. People of Asian heritage make up almost 4 percent of the area's population. That may sound like a small amount, but this racial group grew by 25 percent between 1990 and 2000. Population experts predict that the number of people from Asian Pacific backgrounds will increase quickly in the Tidewater region.

Circle of Life

Northern Virginia is the most racially diverse area of the state. These circle graphs show the percent of people in each racial group there and the percent in the rest of the state.

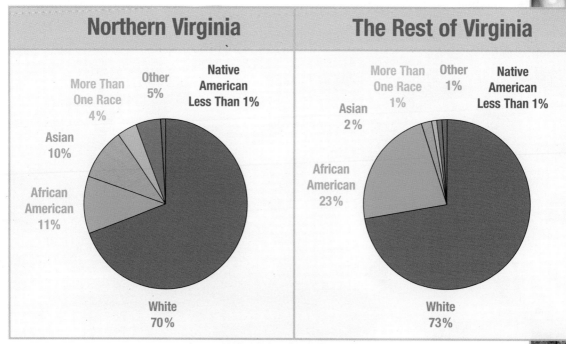

Northern Virginia

- More Than One Race 4%
- Other 5%
- Native American Less Than 1%
- Asian 10%
- African American 11%
- White 70%

The Rest of Virginia

- More Than One Race 1%
- Other 1%
- Native American Less Than 1%
- Asian 2%
- African American 23%
- White 73%

SOURCE: University of Virginia

A young member of the Haliwa-Saponi tribe takes part in a ceremonial dance, held near Charles City, Virginia.

A volunteer teaches English to Asian children who have recently arrived in Arlington, Virginia.

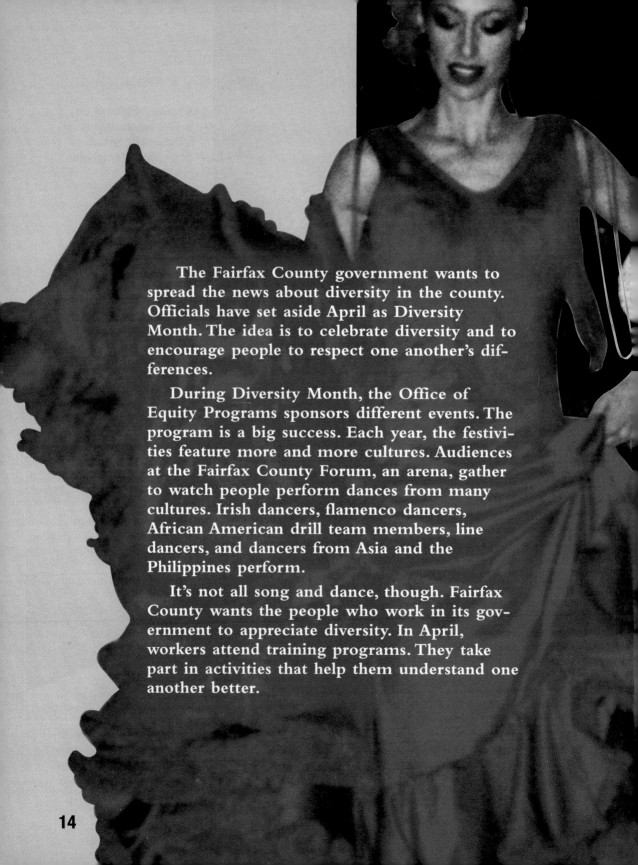

The Fairfax County government wants to spread the news about diversity in the county. Officials have set aside April as Diversity Month. The idea is to celebrate diversity and to encourage people to respect one another's differences.

During Diversity Month, the Office of Equity Programs sponsors different events. The program is a big success. Each year, the festivities feature more and more cultures. Audiences at the Fairfax County Forum, an arena, gather to watch people perform dances from many cultures. Irish dancers, flamenco dancers, African American drill team members, line dancers, and dancers from Asia and the Philippines perform.

It's not all song and dance, though. Fairfax County wants the people who work in its government to appreciate diversity. In April, workers attend training programs. They take part in activities that help them understand one another better.

A flamenco dancer (left) and Kurdish dancers (right) perform at a festival held for Fairfax County Diversity Month.

What's happening in Virginia as it heads toward the next census? Experts say Virginia's growth is slowing down. Why? No one knows for sure. It may have something to do with what is happening in other parts of the United States. The census has shown that the western states are growing in population. Growth in states on the east coast, like Virginia, is slowing down.

That doesn't mean Virginia will stop becoming more diverse. The state has recently started programs to attract a more diverse population. Experts say the state will keep becoming more diverse every year. One thing is for certain—Virginia will always be a state that welcomes everyone.

The cardinal is
Virginia's state bird.